P A P E R J A M

BY

The authors and poets of

The Writers' Hub, Coventry

ISBN: 1499150482

ISBN-13: 978-1499150483

A collection of work
inspired by music and songs

ACKNOWLEDGEMENTS

Thank you for the music, the lyrics and everyone who has inspired us.

Particular thanks go to:
Jo Roberts, for getting *Paper Jam* to a rolling boil, so that we all jelled to produce the anthology;
The Belgrade Theatre for allowing us to meet fortnightly to conserve our ideas;
David Louis for providing the inspiring title and illustration;
Keith Hands for preserving the anthology for posterity;
And to anyone else who knows us!

CONTENTS

The Dark Side of Blackie	*David Louis*	1
The Carnival	*Keith Hands*	5
Bedevilled by Buttons	*Gill Yardley*	6
Loaded	*Russ Berry*	9
Sweet Memories	*Elizabeth Draper*	11
The Day the Wall Came Down	*Simon Grenville*	12
Entrance to a Wood	*Russ Berry*	16
It's Beginning to Look a Lot Like Christmas	*Christine Marsh*	17
Born Without a Twin	*Sarah Menary*	20
Master of the Metal String	*Anna Bradley*	21
Poetry in Motion	*Harminder Sihota*	23
A Grace Note	*David Louis*	24
Writer's Block	*Sarah Meany*	25
The Audition	*Caroline Duffy*	26
The Tapestry Child	*Elizabeth Draper*	30
A Small White Envelope	*David Deanshaw*	32
Moon	*Jo Roberts*	35
Musical Taste	*Jo Roberts*	36
The Hills Were Alive	*Elizabeth Draper*	37
Beethoven Symphony Within	*David Hurt*	39
Sax	*David Hurt*	40
Burn Baby Burn	*Gill Yardley*	41
Bandbox	*Simon Grenville*	44
Black-headed Gull	*Russ Berry*	45
As if they Know	*Jo Roberts*	47
Muse	*Sukhmani Bawa*	48
Madrigal	*David Hurt*	51
Monologue: A Wish	*Sukhmani Bawa*	52
The Future of Air Travel	*Russ Berry*	59
Epitaph	*Keith Hands*	60
The Players	*David Louis*	64
Inspirations for the Collection		65

THE DARK SIDE OF BLACKIE

Time clocked in at: 10am, Saturday, the 11th of the 1st, 2014. I drew in the last long drag on my warm cigarette. I stepped on it and made my dizzy way downstairs to the dingy basement of our covert meeting location. I entered to the eerie shriek of a door creak, and timidly tried to squeeze in a chair between two intimidating and prolific writers. They must have been prolific: their right forearms were immensely muscular. After Irene and Catherine were gracious enough to move their chairs over, I was nestled among the most fearless and dangerous writers that the big bad city of Coventry dared to accept as free-thinking citizens. All staunch anti-smokers, but I reeked of nicotine. I felt their eyeballs all round, aiming at me like mercury injected lead pellets, loaded and poised. I didn't want to overstay my welcome within the first minute, so I slung my duty-free tobacco laden coat as far away as possible, but not before I slipped in an extra strong mint. Alpine fresh and comfortably re-seated, I was ready for another thought provoking session. I'd been tipped off that this one was to be different. Extremely different. We'd all have to actually write something. Their expressions of shock when Jo said that we had to compile an anthology with work from every member, was a sight I shall never forget.

Some nervous twitching and body shifting ensued. To the degree that led to one member leaping up to declare that he had a more pressing Scrabble engagement. We in turn, all breathed a sigh of relief, as his approach to writing in zigzags was puzzling, to say the least.

After he had scurried off with Scrabble bag in hand, and the annoying cacophony of rattling teacups had subsided, Jo proceeded with a suggestion loaded with subliminal suggestiveness. As she leaned to shuffle some cards she mumbled, "We just might need a theme or perhaps a title." We all seized on it, nodding in earnest approval. That's leadership and teamwork!

After some brainstorming, interrupted by the occasional raising of hands, we reached a majority decision on both. Most would call that democracy, others, namely me, mob rule, but an agreement was accepted.

Theme: Music. Title: *Paper Jam*.

The theme of music was inspired by Scrabble man's joyful whistling upon his exit. While making that exit, he had dropped 22 letter pieces and *Paper Jam* was the best title we were able to rustle up from them. It could have been *All that Jazz*, but we were missing one 'z'.

After our meeting had reached its natural conclusion, I stepped up and out from the Belgrade Theatre into a wind-driven day with one calm thought in mind. I knew exactly what I wanted to write. A moment of rare clarity in the midst of an otherwise hazy day. But clarity, my friend, is a writer's best friend, and like a dog, I walked it home; allowing it the odd sniff along the way. Beyond my front door awaited Blackie. Blackie is not my cat, nor my lapdog. Blackie's my old, but faithful laptop. She has black keys, for the curiously minded. She was beckoning me. Mocking me. Challenging me. I courageously accepted, sat down and wrote "Once upon a time". It didn't instantly strike me as a particularly original lead into my first paragraph, but it was a start to my story that, after a few rewrites, read something like this...

I was just a kid whose pocket money couldn't stretch much further than the lining of the pocket it was destined for. There was no way that I could afford a private music teacher. I faced a big problem with no simple solution. That was until I bumped into a cool buddy, who told me that I didn't need a teacher. Tony, a struggling musician of sorts himself, had the cheapest solution. It wasn't the simplest, but upon reflection, it was very sound advice. He said, "Dave, it's all about developing your ear. The best way to learn about music and playing an instrument is to listen, listen and listen some more. Listen to the music that you love until it seeps into you. Music is like a language, but instead of words it's made up of notes. Try to find those on your guitar neck when listening to your favourite musicians, then try to replicate their sound." He also added something that amazed me. It was that top professional guitarists knew the necks of their instruments so intimately that if you were to secretly play a single note anywhere on it, they would know exactly where on the neck that note was produced. They didn't just possess perfect pitch, they had an educated ear for tone.

So far, so good, but I faced another big problem. That moment of rare clarity, the purest thought that I've ever had as a writer; it had vanished like the pen you thought you had nearby when the best sentence that came to mind happened to be the longest and most elusive. But it didn't matter; I'd ample time before the deadline.

The days passed, which began adding up to weeks, before I realised that the *Paper Jam* deadline was now just a day away. I switched on my CD player, set the music, and continued writing, but I still couldn't find my flow. Looking around the room, for some inspiration, I saw it glistening in the reflection of a full bottle of Arthur Bell & Sons' finest. What harm could a little tipple do? While twisting the lid I noticed the reassuring slogan, "Afore ye go." What harm indeed. Besides, if I got too drunk, there was a helpline number on the back of the bottle. I got too drunk and, in my drunken stupor, managed to ring the call centre. My adviser was eloquent, but she only wrote romance. As I wasn't into pure fantasy she recommended a writer in the next cubicle who happened to be brilliant at horror fiction, but he was busy advising a Mr King at great length. I was put on hold, but listening to *Whiskey in the Jar* for the sixth time over no longer amused me.

I hung up, and was about to give up when the percussive intro to AC/DC's *Back in Black* erupted through the speakers. You won't believe this, but something truly spectacular happened. Blackie kicked into gear. I saw her keyboard writing this story for me. Was I hallucinating, or had Blackie noted an email I'd sent enquiring about a sleek tan-sprayed laptop? A new, hot topless model named, Sam Sung, that I was considering replacing her with. In a moment of weakness her hard drive flopped to soft drive as she decided to make herself indispensable and accommodate my every creative whim and fantasy. Whatever her reason, I was witnessing a miraculous writers' partnership.

Her writing wasn't too shabby either. I took the last swig of whisky from the deepest depths of the bottle and hit the stairs running. Scrambling up and down, then down and up repeatedly, until I collapsed and coughed up some sushi of rice paper and jam. "Yeah dude, I needed focus!" But at that point I wanted to see if I could manage to remove the pips that were stuck between my teeth. With my face literally in the mirror I grabbed the floss. Not traditional white floss, but a reel of red cotton thread. That's rock 'n' roll baby! For a brief moment I was in the serenity of dental silence, until the last track on my AC/DC CD shattered it with crashing power chords and screams akin to an un-injected patient having an abscess brutally pierced. The track *Hell ain't a Bad Place* would have been appropriate for that poor patient, but I didn't entirely agree with the sentiment, or the grammar. However, on this occasion, I was willing to compromise, due to my impaired mental faculties and grim real-life circumstances.

I must have blacked out at some point in that song, because I woke up later that morning feeling like a dead man with a deadline looming over his dead head, but at least my teeth were dead clean. Did Blackie finish that story? Yes she did. After a light touch of editing, I reluctantly clicked the email send button. But hold on, why was I worried? All that I needed to say was, "I didn't vote for this slippery theme. I told you that worm breeding would have been a more down-to-earth topic, but you had your heads in the clouds, your ears full of melodies and symphonies. The motion of music swept most of you beyond a table turn." I was going to stick to that statement, in the worst-case scenario: that Blackie's writing, and my editing, simply sucked.

David Louis

THE CARNIVAL

Lights flashing, colours dazzling, shattering my vision.
Bands drumming, sounds exploding, pummeling my hearing.
Moving, spinning, whirling, twisting my consciousness.
Carnival filling my senses, life's excitement surrounding me.

The stilt walker, balancing up high, courting disaster.
The hurdy-gurdy man, winding, singing for everyone.
The acrobats, tumbling, diving, strewing the air with their bodies.
Life condensed, bright, joyous memories flooding me.

Laughing children, crying with joy, overcome by utter happiness.
Hooking ducks, winning prizes, sticky faced with candyfloss.
Walking home, daylight fading, illuminated by deep contentment.
Hands together, one life to another, their love joining mine.

Now it's over, memories evaporate, raindrops in the sunshine.
Regrets, fading with the past, poignant in their resonance.
A distant longing, yearning, for what was, and has gone.
Carnival still fresh and sharp, bittersweet with loss and joy.

Keith Hands

BEDEVILLED BY BUTTONS

The pleasant waitress must have thought me quite strange. My cappuccino, topped by a whirl of chocolate dust, just perfect; the chocolate fudge cake, delicious. My reaction was to look at her in horror. Stifling the urge to be sick, I paid and hurried to the ladies' toilet.

You would be forgiven for thinking this was due to morning sickness or sudden-onset dieter's conscience, in fact the explanation was even stranger. It was simply that, as the girl put my order down, I noticed on the wall opposite a collage made entirely of buttons, and for as long as I can remember I have had a phobia about them.

Even typing the word gives me the creeps. Since I was about four, when others looked under the bed for bogey men, I double-checked the catch on Gran's sewing box, knowing that horrors could roll out of there. I cannot deal with coming across a button unexpectedly, sickness and panic overtake me.

The collage in the teashop was of a penny-farthing bike, made of seemingly hundreds of different shapes, sizes and colours of buttons, and my horror was that one or two might fall off in my direction.

That is the clue to the whole thing, I think. Reliable big sister tells me that when I was three I swallowed a button and choked on it, frightening myself. Gran, wise in the ways of what goes in will follow the plumbing and come out, was not alarmed, saying flippantly, "You'll die after it."

Which I think meant she saw it as a mere hiccup in my digestion, nothing more. Sadly though, it seems to have given me the idea that buttons are dangerous to my safety, and physical sickness and sweating comes on at the sight of any scary ones.

I need to explain, too, that our Mother died when I was one and my sister three, so we had heard and seen what death can do. I think the phrase, 'die after it' has coupled together the words 'death' and 'buttons' in my mind.

It can cause complications. Spiders, rats, snakes, birds — all normal phobias, shared by countless people — can be understood, but buttons! I really do come out in a sweat at the sight of them.

Peculiarly, I use a type of grading system for them too. If one comes off my clothes, I can manage to sew it back on as it is a familiar button, a belonging one. If, however, I put it down to replace later it becomes strange and dangerous. If I find a button where I least expect to I open the door and throw it as far as I can down the garden, holding my breath with my mouth closed, feeling this protects me.

I know from bitter experience that if I throw it in the dustbin I can't rest, and will keep heaving until I'm sick, knowing its whereabouts. I can grade buttons in my mind as to the strength of impact they will have on me. Large black ones are the worst, and any with remaining threads where they have been yanked off will make me almost faint with horror.

Someone else sometimes has to remove them out of sight for me, and my sons have been known to joke about it. However they know better now that it is a genuine phobia with fear and loathing attached. Even the number of holes in buttons perplexes me: two holes are acceptable, and those with eyelets at the back are very civilized, but however much I liked a garment I would not buy it if there were four holes in the buttons on it.

Mostly nowadays there are press studs, zips, and Velcro. Failing that I buy things that button down the back; out of sight, out of mind. I never openly admit to this fear, as I know the world is a button-full place, so there will be problems.

Friends, inviting me over for a meal might be nonplussed at my sudden lack of appetite and visits to the bathroom caused because my radar has sighted an uncovered one on a shelf or fireplace somewhere. They might also wonder which poltergeist placed a card, book, or letter over a dish full of the things: I might still know where they are but can steel myself to stay if they are safely under cover.

I hear the laughter when people say, "Buttons? I think they are lovely!"

or, "How can they hurt you?"

I wish I knew!

I even use it to judge others. If I'm talking to someone who has an odd button sewn on, my opinion of them drops a little and I evade their eyes. Equally I mind very much when one is sewn on with the wrong coloured thread! I suspect the one I swallowed sixty odd years ago might have been pulled off something, and still had its hairy threads showing in its nasty middle.

Writing it down has made me see it more logically, I can recognise the bigger the button the more I panic, and the stray and broken ones (I'm going to be sick again thinking of them) bring me out in a sweat, which makes me get a long way from the sighting.

Which is why, in town, there is one teashop you will never find me in however tempting the fudge cake, however aromatic the coffee.

Gill Yardley

LOADED

Corporal Heaton drew the smoke deep down into her lungs, held it there for several seconds, pushed in the earpiece, hit the volume pad and pressed play. The tiny LCD screen lit up; Primal Scream — *Screamadelica* —1991—track 4; and *Higher Than the Sun* commenced its lysergic sprawl, a panoramic wall of cosmic sound enveloping the afternoon and allowing the corporal a brief respite from the call of duty.

If you could see me now, stood up on the hotel roof in broad daylight you'd take me for a right loony, like that Roman emperor fiddling away while the city burns. But you soon get sick of rushing for cover every time a shell happens to burst over Basra. Call me mental but I reckon it's better to be outdoors where you can see for yourself what's coming your way, get the whole picture. Either that or I've been over here a bit too long.

Heaton flicked away the exhausted spliff, put the leather strap around her neck, closed her left eye and aimed at the horizon, squinting in the late afternoon haze. At this remove, the occasional flashes of fire and muted gunshots from neighbouring towns seemed half-hearted, abstracted, almost languid.

Bulky old thing, heavy too. Looks ancient, like it was last used during the Suez Crisis. Nice bit of kit though. Built to last. Amazing what people leave lying around in the desert ... Shit! It's all a bit fiddly, and I'm not exactly nimble-fingered these days. Keep getting the shakes. Still, a couple more months and I'll be out of here, god willing.

Briefly distracted by the sudden roar as a pair of Tornados shot by, returning to base, Heaton gazed skyward, tracing the contrails in the silence that followed. Then the distant rumble of artillery fire resumed as she turned and made her way back down the steel fire escape, singing harmony accompaniment to the heady gospel opening of *Come Together*.

I'll load it up tonight and nip out before dawn, walk down the old track towards Abadan, maybe shoot some birds at the marshes, see if it works. It's nice and quiet down there with the mist rising up off the water, just like Norfolk really. Might even spot some of those little reed warblers. Just hope I can get the film developed, show them it's not all death and destruction over here. The trick is, you have to find some time for yourself, to do what you want to do, get away from the madness once in a while.

Russ Berry

SWEET MEMORIES

One single red rose
faint perfume lingering
colour quietly fading
slipped between the folds of a silk scarf
lies hidden ……
waiting …….
gentle fingers less nimble with each passing year
softly open the drawer
prompting a quick catch of breath
a flutter of heartbeat
a secret thrill as each fold lifts evoking a warm embrace
releasing a sudden flood of emotive memories,
a table for two
glasses of champagne
sipped under a dark velvet sky peppered with sparkling stars
warm breezes blown in from the sea
ruffle hair and scarf thrown carelessly over one shoulder,
a basket of roses brought to the table
one, selected with care
given with love
accepted with pleasure
anticipation left hanging in the air
words yet unspoken whispering through the rustle of leaves,
on nights such as this
sweet memories are made.

Elizabeth Draper

THE DAY THE WALL CAME DOWN

"Are you working the *Veronica*?"

"Yep."

"And *Gynt*?"

"Yeah."

"What about Festival Ballet? Need a lot of bodies on that one."

"Maybe."

"OK. I'll show you the Green Room."

I walked down the sweet-smelling corridor. It was sweet-smelling because this was a job. A job in a theatre. I was about to be inducted as a day man in a musical. A Day Man! It meant I was paid a daily rate to work the show. And this was a big show with two TV stars — older and greyer and moving more slowly than you remembered them, but people from the telly. The Telly! And it seemed like a hundred dancers, lithe and lean and glistening under the umbrella of stage lights. And they needed an extra day man!

And I got the job! Me!

Moving scenery that smelt of glue. Stage weights ice cold to the touch.

Straining at ropes with blistered hands. Blistered-blue hands.

And gaffer tape that screamed at you as you unfurled it.

And there was a Green Room. Where the actors lived.

Real actors. Proper actors. Paid actors. This-was-their-main-job-actors, with beads and scarves and cigarettes delicately balanced on middle fingers and talking non-stop. Non-stop natter I called it. They talked posh and their hair was brushed clean. I didn't see how I could ever join this gang. They played Scrabble and sophisticated word games. They laughed deep-throated laughs. And were always happy. Some of them talked about film!

"I played Red Indian in the Nevada Desert for three months. Stinking pay! I must have been good: I couldn't recognise myself on screen."

"I did three months," said Jeff standing beside me. We'd come in for our break. He was small and squat and perfectly proportioned like a manqué's dummy with dapper biceps and a Zappa moustache that was the height of fashion then.

"Three months," I said. "What in?"

"Winson Green," he said. "D-wing. GBH Aggravated. That's when I went Sikh."

"Sikh?"

"Yeah. See, if you change your religion they have to let you grow your hair. You get special food. And that really got up their noses, seeing me walk round with long hair, every other twat forced to have a crew cut."

"But within the year she was in bed with his gardener!"

"Johnny's wife? With the gardener? How very Lawrencian!"

"Course it couldn't last. They grabbed me coming out the showers, held me down, shaved me clean dry, bone dry "

"I still get residuals from Korea. Framed the cheque darling, framed the cheque."

And the smells: the smelly-welly sweat from the stage hands, and then that funny money smell of stage make-up, No 5 and No 9, like linseed oil and Pond's cold cream, and sodden tissues discarded like confetti, and hair lacquer lavishly sprayed and hanging in the air, catching in your lungs like cling film.

And the crackle of fresh-ironed cotton and happy-clappy heels on cold room corridors and always that same bloody song.

It's the End of an Age, Anne Veronica, it's the End of an Age.

You get spat on a lot as a stage hand. It's a fact. The sopranos and tenors meet together in a spray of spittle that falls over you like snow.

Wet snow. It's because you're up-close, crouched down, smelling the smooth polished wooden stage. A raked stage they call it, where the dancers dance and the singers sing and the stage hands sweat...

So there I was, squatting behind No 10 Downing Street ready to move it into centre stage the moment the suffragettes came on in a sea of green and spit. But we were good. Like clockwork our scene changes...

Tick-tock. Tick-tock.

And Stella the stage manager, in control at all times.

The Robot we called her.

"Great tits!"

Harsh black-rimmed spectacles and hair scraped back into a tight-clipped bun, a slight beginning of grey, even at 26. That strident arresting walk, attacking the pavement. Faded blue-denim jacket splattered with paint and buttons missing. Her arms held against her chest like a weapon.

Like me, she had a yen to go to drama school and, like me, she failed audition after audition. And then one day, during *Peer Gynt*, she got in! And so did I. She went to Bristol and I went to Kent. I had Lamorebey Park in summer and she had Clifton Suspension Bridge in winter. Bound together in ambition.

And on the last night of *Kiss Me Kate* her hair was out of its bun, dropping onto her shoulders like chiffon. Chiffon caught in a summer's breeze. Her walk more relaxed. The limbs languid. The jacket hanging loose. We chatted and she offered me a spliff and I said I'd have one later. And I did.

And in the warmth of the stale darkness, standing close by the prompt corner, out of sight of all comers, I felt the heat of her body against mine and together we touched hands briefly and I knew it then. The wall had come down.

That evening was like meeting my soul sister. Up till then I had known only sex. This was something different. This was sharing and surrendering and blissful and giving and loving and watchful and waking and never stopping and free from anxiety and other stuff I can't explain.

Next morning I woke sweat-laden, drenched in your phonemes. Drenched like a mermaid swimming in the ocean sea of lust.

You dressed with such casual ease that morning, as if nothing had happened. How did you do that? How could you leave with just a blown kiss and a silently slammed door? How?

Stell, I love you still-always-and for ever. (Of course you know this.)

See. For me it's this simple: that summer, I worked the *Veronica*.

Simon Grenville

ENTRANCE TO A WOOD

Impulse draws you onto an unmarked road
Through orchards soft and rank with windblown fruit,
On a whim, a sudden change of mood
Without a map or care for any route;
You brush against the hedgerows as you march
By sandstone walls and through a corner gate
And further down a lane, behind a church,
A standing stone; an entrance to a wood
Where hazel boughs converge into an arch.
You push aside a scrub of broom and cut
Across a timbered thicket to a brook,
Green beds of lichen springing underfoot.
Then down a bank to a cloistered nook
Where hazel limbs are hung with scarlet blossom,
All coiled in woollen yarn and twists of rag:
A leaden silence takes you to its bosom.
You sit distracted on a mossy log
And scan the static trees, the silent birds.
Your brain grows wild; your jaw begins to sag
And bursts with golden laughter, conjured words;
Faces in the bracken, silver in the well,
Rags on the hazel, the music on the hill
Where devils play pipes and whistles.
The buzzing limes, the healing springs,
The sylvan tongues of old green men
Grinning, gurning in the hedgerow.
Emerging by the entrance to the lane;
Moonlight through the arch, the standing stone,
Here on your hands, the vinifera stain
And all the while you thought you were alone.

Russ Berry

IT'S BEGINNING TO LOOK A LOT LIKE CHRISTMAS

As Amanda made her way home from school she could feel little flutters in her tummy, she was so excited. It was nearly Christmas and the day after next she would be on holiday for nearly three weeks. Today though, was all about the Christmas tree. Yesterday her dad and her brother Tom had fetched the traditional decorations down from the loft and she'd selected the ones she wanted to use. As soon as her dad had finished work they were all going to meet him at the garden centre to buy the tree, tinsel, crêpe paper and glitter, so that Amanda and her mum could re-dress the fairy and make new tree decorations — as they did every year. Amanda already had some really good ideas because this week her comic had two pages showing how to make Christmas decorations. The more she thought about it the more excited she felt. This was almost her favourite part of Christmas, although it was difficult to pick a favourite, because everything about Christmas was magical.

She knew her mum had been baking before she opened the kitchen door as she could smell the familiar spicy scents of Christmas cooking. Mum was always baking lovely biscuits and cakes but at Christmas the smells were more delicious. A few weeks ago she could smell the Christmas cake and mincemeat cooking before she had even opened the garden gate and it all added to the excitement. Mum was in the kitchen and had just taken out of the oven a tray of golden, sugared small cakes in paper cases that had "Merry Christmas" printed on them. Her mum hugged her and gave her a big kiss, whilst promising she could have one of the mince pies she'd baked as soon as they had cooled down a little. Amanda went upstairs to change. Hanging up on her wardrobe door was her new party dress. The skirt was like a shimmering rainbow and her Mum had sewn sequins onto the top so that it sparkled. She couldn't wait to wear it to the party tomorrow.

When she got back downstairs her mum had a mince pie and a drink waiting for her and her brother Tom. "Eat up! We need to get going soon," said her mum, "and we have lots to do when we get back." It was only a short ride in Mum's car and when they pulled into the car park Dad was already waiting for them. While Tom and his dad headed for the big yard where all the trees were kept, Amanda and her mum went in search of glitter, tinsel and crêpe paper.

The crêpe paper was in so many different colours, Amanda didn't know which to choose. Last year she had chosen pink crêpe paper and silver glitter. Everything looked beautiful so it was a difficult choice, but in the end she decided to make the fairy a white skirt with a gold top and decorate both with gold and silver glitter. Her mum agreed with her, and they bought everything they needed and a bit more, just in case, even though they knew from experience that there would be enough and some left over. They decided that this year the tree would be decorated in white and gold so they added some more tinsel and some pretty gold and silver wrapping paper to cover the top of table the tree would stand on.

With everything bought, Tom and Dad squashed the tree into Dad's car. There was only just enough room in the back for Tom and they set off home with the tree tickling Tom's head. Amanda went with her mum and held the big bag carefully all the way home, so as not to squash the crêpe paper. Her dad and Tom were already home and potting the tree in the tub when Amanda and her mum arrived. "Dinner in five minutes" her mum called to them. "I just need to reheat the stew so we have plenty of time to start decorating the tree." Amanda couldn't wait. She put everything she would need together onto the big front room table, including the cardboard and match boxes that had taken her weeks to collect.

After dinner, Dad and Tom went to finish potting up the tree leaving mum and Amanda to get started on dressing the fairy. Amanda's mum had long ago made a cardboard pattern for the fairy's crêpe dress. The bottom of the dress was really only a circle with a hole in the centre but it was just the right size. They always made sure that the pattern was packed safely away in the same box as the decorations after Christmas, so that they knew where it would be the next year. Amanda carefully cut out the skirt from crêpe paper following the cardboard pattern. Her mum sewed little running stitches around the centre circle and Amanda then gathered them to make little pleats. Once the top had been cut out from the gold paper her mum helped her fit it to the fairy. It was very fiddly as the fairy was quite small. Now it was time for the glitter, the part that Amanda loved. All the fairy needed then was a sprinkling of fresh glitter onto her wings and her clean net skirt tied over the top. They agreed this year the fairy looked more beautiful than ever.

While mum went to prepare the table ready for the tree, Amanda started to make her other decorations. Copying the instructions in her comic, and using all the treasures she had collected, she made little lanterns, stars, baskets, drums and bows. When the table had been finished, mum helped Amanda fill the matchboxes with sweets and little gifts, then covered them in the crêpe paper sprinkled with glitter. The finishing touch was a tinsel bow and loop so they could hang on the tree. Her dad and brother brought the tree in and put it onto the table ready to decorate. With everyone helping it took no time at all. Amanda noticed her brother whispering to Dad — it had something to do with the shed — and they both disappeared. Amanda was puzzled but finished hanging the last of the decorations just as they came back in carrying a basket.

They all admired the decorated tree but knew it wouldn't look its best until the fairy was on the top. "We have something special this year," Dad said smiling and Tom showed them the basket of fir cones that they had sprayed silver. "This is our contribution to the Christmas tree" said Tom proudly. They found spaces for all the fir cones and Dad carefully lifted the fairy onto the top of the tree. There were just the lights left to do, and Amanda couldn't wait till they were switched on. "Right," said Dad, plugging them in. "Shall we count down to switch on?" Mum turned off the main light and they all counted down: five, four, three, two, one. Dad flicked the switch and they all cheered when the lights burst into colour. Amanda gazed at the colours reflecting off all the decorations she had made. "Oh, this is the best Christmas tree ever!" she said. They all laughed as she said the same every year. "Yes," said Dad, "now it's really beginning to look a lot like Christmas."

Christine Marsh

BORN WITHOUT A TWIN

Born without a twin,
My heart is cut asunder,
Wrenched limb from limb,
Forever lost.

I am replaced always,
Night after night,
Days upon days,
By people that forget my name.

Falling deeper into grey shadow,
And eternal obscurity,
Lonely as the crow,
I yearn for you.

Friend I will never know,
My mirror in every way,
Our bond will grow,
Deeper for never knowing you.

Sister who should have been,
One day we will be whole,
I search for you eternally in my dreams,
Together in the hereafter.

Sarah Menary

MASTER OF THE METAL STRING

Granddad was master of the metal string. He pinged it. It was his rusty music, his cry for help. Imagine a guitar string fingered on repeat. That was just the sound of Granddad, plucking his hospital bed while his lopsided mouth churned an inward chorus and he tried to tap out a Morse code with his index finger. He would lie, like a strange idiot, listening to institutional rolls and hisses, looking at his patch of white wall, the one a silvery pool of light hit, and made glow. It was a perfect circle of happiness.

I remember when we used to sit in a field of grass, putting wide reeds between two thumbs, exhaling into that tiny space. I had soft bones and could fit the sun between my thumb and forefinger. Now I know that that is one trick amongst many, just like the moonlight made Granddad see Grandma in the shadows from his metal bed; that was a trick too. What a little moonlight can do.

Before life's edges hardened, there were perfect circles of happiness everywhere. My brother and I used to tease him but it was the kind of teasing Granddad just laughed at. Granddad and Grandma stood there, stalwart against an ivory sun. When it was the nurses laughing at him and his gobbledygook it wasn't so pretty. Oh, but you haven't heard the velvet words of his youth, I wanted to say, but tried to think of a way of saying it so they didn't giggle at me too. I wondered what game I would have to play to get them to love him.

The other day I came with Mum. We brought some flowers. He chanted his shadowy hello. His skin looked like dry biscuits and I asked myself when those authoritative cheeks had turned so shallow. The reflective landscape of the hospital couldn't accommodate him anymore. He looked as though he would flake away if I touched him, so I just stood there, his metal strumming the musical backdrop.

So that I could remember him with enduring dignity I closed my eyes and thought of the time we sat in a field of grass. The sun came out and identified some wildflowers and beginnings of other buds, differentiated them from the grass. What a little sunlight can do.

The nurses stopped laughing, the finger stopped pinging.

Anna Bradley

POETRY IN MOTION

My love he was a hound dog,
He never committed any serious crime,
The police thought he was on the rob,
They always had suspicious minds.

I can't help falling in love with him,
As I saw him in the dock,
I think he was all shook up,
When they sentenced him to jailhouse rock.

My letters were returned unopened,
He sent back my blue suede shoes,
I cried, "What have I done to deserve this?
Please, please, don't be cruel!"

My dear, are you lonesome tonight?
It's always on my mind,
I watched An American Trilogy,
Which you had left behind.

The day he was released,
I said, "It's now or never,
I love the wonder of you,
Just as you think King Creole is clever."

At Heartbreak Hotel we meet,
He apologies for 'return to sender',
A request for a little less conversation,
As he wants to love me tender.

I'm sick of living in the ghetto,
If I can dream it can really make us,
Marry me and become my wife,
And let's head off to viva Las Vegas.

Harminder Sihota

A GRACE NOTE

Dear Santa

My name is Grace and I am aged seven and nearly a half. I'm always in a dream. Not always really but most of the time. Here I am standing in front of our hallway mirror again dreaming of the one thing I dream about most of. Only my mirror knows about what that dream is about. And it helps me with my dream. Right then I was standing with my violin in my arms like I would hold my teddy bear called Muzzier. That is a funny name I know because it tickles me every time I say it. I am sure it is the one you gave to me last Christmas. Sometimes I play my pretend violin like my mother plays her violin. But her one is bigger and she keeps it locked in her violin case in her locked music room. She always says that it is far too expensive and big for me to play. But when I hear her play on it it is so beautiful that it makes me cry most of the times. I dream about being as good as my mother one day. But I cannot get started. My mother's playing can send me and Muzzier to sleep sometimes and when she does I dream that I am a very good violin player and Muzzier dances to my own tunes. He is really funny when he dances. He does this spin that is so fast I can never see his face anymore. And then he stops spinning slowly and falls back down. I have to stop playing when that happens because we both wake up in a cuddle. So here is what I would really really love to have. A little violin that is all my very own size and some tiny dancing shoes for Muzzier.

My mother says that to thank you in advance.

Grace and Muzzier. x x

David Louis

WRITER'S BLOCK

He lived on a diet of coca cola,
And Skittles.

He called himself a vampire,
The writer.

Bags under his eyes, grey against
The blood-shot pink,
He did not sleep.

Stories whirring in his head,
Colliding like exploding dervishes.

But worse...

The writer's block.

Pens chewed to the wick,
Hair ripped out, brains picked clean,

And his victim, the computer,
Defenestrated.

Sarah Menary

THE AUDITION

The taxi stopped abruptly just past the tall cast iron gates. In her haste to get out she didn't stop for change from the incomprehensible driver. Standing on the pavement in the dimming light, she looked back at number 22. This was a wealthier part of the city but the tall Georgian building loomed some distance from other properties. It was surrounded by fir trees. An old sign hidden in the overgrown shrubs passed unnoticed — the Embassy of Contigua.

The old gate was chained allowing just enough space to push through. The unkempt grounds and broken windows gave away that it had long ago fallen into disrepair. A handwritten sign, *Café Yama – Auditions* pointed to the lower ground floor. Old limestone steps led down, cold, grey and worn, and each step brought reality closer, her heartbeat quickened. How would this audition go? Who would be present? Breathing deeply to keep her nerves in check, Carmen felt she was moving closer to her renewed singing career with each step. The light from the street reduced as dusk fell around. Pools of earlier rain were starting to freeze in the cracks as the temperature dropped. Taking hold of the rail (rusted in parts) to steady and guide her down, she arrived at the bottom step. The warmth of the Whole Earth Café near the Notting Hill tube station and the aroma of fresh coffee against the background of Latin American drum beats a distant rumble.

The entrance was located under an arch in an alcove. Brambles like barbed wire and dead flowers lay straggled across the doorstep; she cleared them with her foot. Pulling the ivy back from the large old oak door. She knocked. Rustling nervously in her handbag she fished out the invitation, she had been so focused on her performance, her appearance that she had not read the details thoroughly. As she pulled out the letter, she dropped her music sheets on the floor — *Las Liberates* by A Onterata. The invitation stated clearly Café Yama with the full address. The RSVP had been a messaging service; not unusual as demand for auditions like this were high. The door creaked eerily as it opened, a rush of dust blew up from the floor. She stepped back allowing it to escape, she could not risk an asthma attack. Her long full taffeta gown rustled against the broken floor tiles.

A glimmer of light cast a shadow across the hall. Small cobwebs hanging down from high ceilings blew in from an unknown draught and the light caught the shimmer on her long diamante earrings. Her "Hello" resounded in the gloom. The weighted front door slammed shut behind her its sound echoing across the hallway with a deep resonance. Adjusting her eyes to the dimness she noticed that the light came from small windows at the far end of the large room — the glass was thick with pollutants and grime, the outside light seemed to be reflected from small dust particles which floated in the air. Transfixed, she stopped for a moment. She had been distracted and surprised by her surroundings but her nerves were slowly settling. She should have researched the details before coming. After many years, she had almost given up hope of resuming her singing career and she had been so ecstatic to receive a request to audition at Café Yama that she had not completed the usual checks. What was she thinking? Café Yama had sounded so exotic then, but now she shuddered.

The café had been set up some years ago for the many refugees fleeing the revolution in Contigua, but was unknown to Carmen. Dirty unused chairs and tables were stacked in the far corners, curled posters on the wall spelling out a menu long past its sell by date. People who fled as refugees wanted to forget, so this café had quickly lost its clientele. In the poor light, Carmen could just make out the remnants of a cello which lay in the centre of the room, splintered, fragmented and stained with darkened blood. She gasped. Her body slumped at this sight and then again as she noticed a stooped figure. "Alberto!" She bowed low and tears of days long forgotten began to fall as moved with outstretched arms towards him. There, in this dimly lit room Alberto Onterata sat. He was now so old he could barely stand without the assistance of a stick, yet his intense focused eyes were able to see into the depths. A legendary world-renowned composer who had fled, one of the *desaparecer* (the disappeared), was here present at Café Yama.

He smiled weakly; a faint, "Carmen – look at you!" His frail hands lifted as if to frame her face "Bella, please." He gesticulated towards the centre of the room where the cello and a single microphone, lit as if by a spotlight, were placed. As he waved the recital papers, he added finally one final word as he looked straight into her eyes: "Remember." He pointed to the spot where she was to audition.

Then, sensing someone else in the room, she turned her gaze. There, lit by candlelight, the grand piano hidden in the shadows of the room seemed restored to its former glory, although in the flickering candlelight faint scars could be seen across its legs. Sat at the piano was Solomon, eyes shining with determination. Solomon Lomas, carved out a tune as smoke twirled from a long cigar in his mouth, a slow smile and a nod. This sight brought laughter into the room. He first ran through the scales then onto the music sheets and *Las Liberates* began to unfold. He nodded, his voice — a deep gravelly tone following years of smoking yet strangely sensitive — pleaded, "Carmen take us away!"

Mesmerised, hypnotised by the timing, the ease with which the notes fell into place, Carmen could almost hear the sound of the cello coursing through the air as the piano's notes unravelled lower and lower and then stopped. Her cue. She remembered.

"*Las Liberates*! Viva, Carmen! Viva la noche!" they had chanted as the performance began. The show that had never finished. An audience in all its finery had been cut down in its prime. Brutal, cruel and cowardly.

Death and decay all around, a stench of burned bodies, the pungent smell of incendiary devices, the executions in the streets. The blood curdling screams. That dreadful night had been the last time she had sang to a full opera house. In the streets, the carnage was evident as people fled the theatre screaming, stumbling and numb. The 6th July 1976 had seen Contigua annexed to the larger neighbouring state.

Back in the present, she connected with the memories, blood red rage flowed through her veins. Her voice soared to new levels as she remembered how the bludgeon came down on the cello, the butchery of those in the orchestra, her fiancée, Roberto, dying on the stage.

Connecting with her unexpressed grief she felt the restraints and shackles that had imprisoned her for years fall away. Unburdened and lighter she hit the highest A. Her voice was flying free through the air borne by her deeply held belief that her people too would one day know this freedom. Their spirit, although broken, would be rebuilt by this new production directed by Solomon, its powerful lyrics bringing alive the love she had once felt.

As she finished her recital, the room was filled with a new energy and life. As she bowed low to the short staccato applause, they were all in tears but not for long. Life had been kinder to her; the age and frailty of her compatriots was evident.

Alberto turned to Carmen. "The role is yours — you will be Gabriella once again." Gabriella was the feisty saviour of *Las Liberates*, the opera that had become an anthem of defiance. Realisation of what she had accomplished began to sink in. She would lead and represent her country at the *Viva la Noche* festival.

Solomon poignantly explained, "We will never forget them, Carmen. This recital will be for those who lost their lives. They will never be forgotten." The funds raised from the performance would contribute to the education of those who had fled, so that Contigua's music and culture would never die.

The front door seemed strangely lighter as she pulled it open, and the blast of fresh air that greeted her had an almost ethereal quality. The huge white full moon which had risen high in the sky lit the deep indigo night. Carmen breathed deeply again and started her ascent towards the stars, still humming the final chorus line: *Las Liberates — Viva la noche!*

Caroline Duffy

THE TAPESTRY CHILD

The weaver of dreams
has a dream to weave
for the tapestry child
waiting high on the hill
looking out on a landscape
so grey and so bare
with the belching of chimneys
polluting the air
not a bird in the sky
nor a fish in the sea
not a green blade of grass
nor a leaf on a tree
can rise from these ashes of disharmony
till you tapestry child
hang your threads in the sky
to wait for that moment
the warmth from the sun
releases the colours
your dream has begun.

Now the weaver of dreams
And the spinner of yarns
sees the tapestry child
gather threads in each hand
throwing high in the air
to be caught by a breeze

carried far on the wind
from these threads of creation
the patchwork begins
spreading colour and light
over once barren land
weaving seeds of new growth
through a circle of hands.

Now the tapestry child
waits high on the hill
looks out on a landscape
of colour and life
hears music and laughter
where once was all grey
but the weaver of dreams
has slipped quietly away.

Elizabeth Draper

A SMALL WHITE ENVELOPE

It was just an ordinary square white envelope. The address had been typed onto a label — so I was one of many to receive them. It was stiff; it obviously contained a small card — an invitation perhaps? Was I expecting anything? I recognised the postmark. It came from where she lived!

Love letters straight from your heart; keep us so near while apart.

The memories came flooding back ...

For the first time in our lives, we had begun to understand the term 'soul-mate'.

Then I recalled that together we had made a shameful decision many years earlier. We could have returned and undone the wrong, but we both blamed each other.

Perhaps it was the enormity of that decision, or the fact that we would have difficulty facing each other, knowing what we had done, that had blown us apart. We had seemed to be so much in love. This was to have been the great love of our lives and we had made such a major decision so quickly and without thinking of the consequences.

Then my job took me 200 miles away, but we stayed in touch — on paper.

After that, we had gone our separate ways, despite attempts by me to restore what was lost. So deep was this loss that I had started to write about it. Would it be a novel, laced with creative licence? Or would it be autobiographical? So strong had my feelings been for her that I had kept all her letters, locked away in the loft in an old cardboard shoe box. There were photographs too, as well as one truly poignant feature — a receipt for a dozen red roses with the message, "Please come back." All of this was to no avail.

After over 30 years of heartache I had the time and capacity to mount a search for her. But was it really to be? Three firms of private detectives had drawn blanks. Had they tried hard enough? Or was it just an instance of the old adage: "If you want something done properly, do it yourself!"?

Eventually, I found her. Then, like opening Pandora's Box without thinking, I found that only hope remained.

I learned to my dismay that her past few years had been spent living in a tied cottage with second-hand furniture, working for a charity. That's where she'd met Ted. Her job had been to stimulate the minds of these old folk; he had been one of them. She tried to help them to remember the good times and support them when the sad memories got the better of them. She was a kind woman. She too had loved and lost many times in her life. Most of all with me all those years ago, or so she told me. When briefly I'd arrived back in her life she was overjoyed at first, then, when she realised that my marriage was solid, complained with some sadness that I was just clearing my conscience. Perhaps we could have been happy if she had not driven me away. She also said that she had loved me all those years ago, but she had made the decision to send me away. Why? Because I could not be faithful and I just could not resist temptation.

Now it looked like she was going to get married again — and once again not to me.

It was probably to Ted. I had met Ted, a widower, a couple of times. Ted was a dour man with a north Lancashire accent which seemed a strangely foreign sound — even in west Merseyside where the Scouse dialect is so strong.

Why had she chosen Ted? Security probably — not the emotional type of course, but probably financial. Of course I hoped she would be happy, secure, comfortable and content.

Was it to be a big do? Did I really want to go?

I fingered the envelope, almost not wishing to open it, turning it over and over again, thinking and remembering. Perhaps I should just send a cheque with best wishes and then forget about her completely, just as I had had been forced to do, 40 years earlier. What would be the point of being there in the church listening to her being given away, again? But not to me.

I reached for the silver letter opener — a gift from her all those years ago. It was still in pristine condition, in its original box, in my desk. The notelet, covered with roses, that said "with love" had been lost — it was only a scrap of paper and my desk had been moved many times over 40 years. But the letter opener had come from her so it would remain with me forever.

I turned the envelope over so as not to face the address and stamp. I inserted the silver blade slowly and with trepidation. Could she really be marrying Ted, of all people?

I was right. It was a card carrying an invitation.

I read the contents. A lump rose in my throat. The tears that I had expected burned in the back of my eyes before cascading down my cheek.

Yes I would send a cheque.

I could not bear the thought of her lying there in her coffin.

But I still have all her letters.

David Deanshaw

MOON

I would give you the moon if I could,
not on a stick
but place it in your trusting hands
a harvest moon fat and round,
an amber moon that glows
as bright as a jar of honey in late summer.

I would give you the stars if I could,
not in a box
but wrapped inside a navy night
so when they wake from infinite slumber
you could watch the starlight bloom.

I would give you the universe if I could,
not all of it
just between infinity and here
so you could feel the ancient weight of it,
measure days in galaxies
and your life in eternal discovery.

Jo Roberts

MUSICAL TASTE

If music is supposed to be the food of love
then ply me with a taste of Beethoven,
an uplifting aria perhaps.
I'm not a fussy eater.
A bite of Bach might assuage my appetite
or I can nibble round the edges of some Chopin
while I'm waiting.
Just don't offer me a Mozart prelude,
I much prefer the zest of Rimsky Korsakov unless
you can find a morsel of Satie to satisfy me.
Also nothing overdone
as that would sit heavy with me for days,
so please no Rosetti requiem on the menu.
Mind you for a change, just a few bars from anything
by Hildegard of Bingen might be welcome.
Not everyone's cup of tea agreed,
liturgical chant does have a tendency to repeat.
I'll pass on the nouveau cuisine of John Adams,
although a soupçon of Arvo Pärt would go down a treat.
But if you really love me,
make my taste buds dance with Debussy.

Jo Roberts

THE HILLS WERE ALIVE

Cowbells are as much a part of alpine culture as yodelling and the Lederhosen. They keep herds of cattle together on the mountain pasture as they graze the herbage. Of course it's one of the traditions we've come to expect and enjoy during holidays in the Alps. This time we were staying in the Swiss hamlet of Barboleuse a short mountain train ride from Villars.

It was early June, a perfect month for alpine flowers, with some still emerging from their winter blanket of snow. The hills were alive that fine spring day as the orchestrated sound of bells was carried on the wind.

We had made for Les Diablerets, taking the first cable car of the summer season to the Refuge d'Isenau. At the top station we found a spot on the sun-drenched terrace surrounded by a panoramic view of mountains. In the keen, clear air, a mug of hot chocolate was a perfect body warmer.

It was soon time to move off in the direction of Lac Retaud. The path took us through an alpine paradise that any ardent plant enthusiast would die for. Spring gentians, a vivid blue at our feet; its cousin the grand yellow gentian, a spire of large golden star-like flowers; red dwarf rhododendron clinging to rocky outcrops. Flowers stretched in every direction. Far below in the valley the harmonious clanging of cow bells completed this alpine idyll. After an hour's walking we found a smooth rock providing a perfect view of the lake and munched our sandwiches.

We circled the sweep of water and quickly losing height found ourselves at the lower station of a cable car. The serenity of the day was interrupted by the clamour of voices and the whirring of machinery as the cable cabin started on its aerial journey. Its destination Glacier 3000 was spelt out in large letters on the side of the cabin itself.

Leaving this intrusion behind, we headed for the forest. The tortuous footpath through the pine trees led us past a cascading waterfall. Up and down, in and out, under and over fallen tree trunks. After half an hour of following the river forever leading us down and down, we came to flower meadows again and the first chalets of the village. We had arrived at Diablerets.

A day later on the path to Chemin de l'Eau with the promise of it being another delightful day under a cloudless sky, we made our way through meadows of long grass and woodland forest to picnic in a clearing. We were now used to the clanging of bells, that familiar musical sound, that unique harmony of chords.

A short walk on the road towards Bretaye, then back on a path through alpine meadows towards Les Ecouvets. We were blissfully unaware of the danger lurking around the corner.

The pastoral scene was peaceful enough. A herd of Swiss brown horned cattle lifted their heads to stare with soft brown eyes while placidly chewing the long luscious grass.

The musical clanging of bells continued while they stood like sentinels on both sides of the path keeping a watchful eye. We stopped to take a photograph and immediately without warning they began to move towards us. Tossing heads and stamping hooves, the clanging of their bells drowned out by menacing bellows. The herd was about to break into a gallop. It was time to move on. To move on quickly. But no, they would soon outrun us, so we took our chance to make our stand, waving arms and shouting. Thankfully the stampede came to an abrupt halt. It was our chance to escape.

A half-walk half-run across the meadow took us out of danger and onto another path. As we emerged from the last meadow we reached a clearing. There was our car, now in the midst of a family barbecue. Swiss families busily cooking supper. With a smile and a "bon appetit" it was time to make our way back to our chalet in Barboleuse.

The hills maybe alive with the sound of cow bells, but beware of belligerent horned cattle wearing them!

Elizabeth Draper

BEETHOVEN SYMPHONY WITHIN

Its synchronism reverberated and stimulated every atom of his inner being,
until its secret poured out and painted beauty on to paper.

His canvas, to his art.

It then plagued him to be performed,
it needed to be heard.

It was passionate, vigorous, theatrical, moving and complex.

A masterpiece,
an epic ambition,
a mission to stun and perplex,
yet enquire and enthral.

His inner being had fine hearing.

His masterpiece
was right to plague him.
to be performed
to be heard...

David Hurt

SAX

Its saffron cues beat with lissom feet.
Lissom feet that jive the echoes of ragtime roots
And hint the vibes of heart and soul.
Lifting spirits to a breezy tone,
Relaxed and carefree.

David Hurt

BURN BABY BURN

It was a fishy business. The lying in state took 10 hours; around 500 people filed past the body to pay respect, dressed in black, sobbing loudly. Men, women, motley priests and popes vented their grief at the loss of their loved one: ten foot of aquamarine glitter, with lobster bisque lipstick round its pouting mouth and red eyes that lit up as it got dark. It was the 'Funeral for the Sardine', Tenerife carnival style.

Excitement mounted as darkness fell and the time for the cremation came near. The weeping and wailing got louder. A solemn band headed up the cortège, with people playing instruments badly and loudly, followed by a procession of widows with black lacy mantilla weeds veiling their faces, priests, lots of men in drag having the time of their lives, and a motley collection of children dressed in fancy dress. We were 'blessed' many times by false clergy and invited to kiss crucifixes whilst we waited for the whole spectacle to start.

Somewhere in the throng was the annually visiting German band, dressed like people on a Quality Street box or the Child Catcher from Chitty Chitty Bang Bang, with red and white feathered plumage coming out of top hats, long white coats pinned at the back of their legs by small brass buttons, oompah-ing all the way through the pretty streets of Puerto de la Cruz to the dear departed's final destination at the fishing harbour. There it was ceremonially cremated on a funeral pyre, watched over by the bronze statue of a Tinerfena fishwife with a basket of live fish on her head, and a bucket in her right hand, the fish flying to escape. The cinders from the fire floated through the air as the smell of sulphur and wood smoke mingled with the fishy sea smell of the harbour wall. It all added to the excitement.

This was followed by a firework display, and a grand ball in the town square that went on long into the night. It was Ash Wednesday and sardines used to be the main trade of Tenerife; also the Christian symbol is a fish, so we made some assumptions that were not confirmed — we were just told it is an old custom.

It is partying full on, with two weeks of celebrations to enjoy, involving all the inhabitants of Puerto de la Cruz, and beginning with a night-time carnival procession. There were fancy dress competitions galore, this year the theme was Minnie Mouse for the girls, and Wild West for the boys. Many and varied were the interpretations of this. The choosing of the carnival queen was free and very public, and there were dance displays and a ball in the main square, Plaza del Charco, nearly every night.

Another interesting tradition is 'Kill the snake', an event which happened at various points during the day and was billed as a custom from the old traditional Puerto de la Cruz carnival. There was a men's marathon in high heels on another night, when the dress was outrageous and we were invited to squeeze a flat chest encircled by a black basque with red lace trim, with a lot of black chest hair poking out. All part of the fun, of course.

On the serious side, there was an exhibition of rally cars on the seafront, with immaculate Cadillacs, Pontiacs, Chevrolets, and one lone Austin Seven to keep Britain's side up. Police blew on whistles to stop people touching the fine machines, and the immaculate vehicles drew more oohs and aahs than the oompah band at the funeral of the dear departed sardine.

The two weeks ended with a five-hour parade through the streets, where the waiting staff from our hotel were spotted in Hawaiian shirts, and the chambermaids did their bit in fancy dress too. Everything is free, and safe, with no warnings of muggings or crime. The Carnival extravaganza marks the beginning of Lent — next year this will be the two weeks beginning 7th February to 21st February, with the burning of the sardine taking place on 18th February 2015.

Tenerife traditionally made its living from sardines, prior to tourism, so possibly this is why they grieve the passing of a paper one, though it is part of the fun of the yearly carnival that attracts tourists from all over the world, and some say is second only to Rio. It is certainly Europe's largest pre-Lent activity, and very colourful too. There is also a high-heeled drag race through the narrow rocky streets, up and down steps, runners urged on by the crowd. There are nightly street parties, dancing till dawn and heaven only knows how your waiter will be dressed in the morning!

Puerto de la Cruz is at the top of the island of Tenerife, green, lush, and rocky. Not quite as warm as the south, it makes up for this by being tropical in nature, as well as having more historical sites to visit. This part of Tenerife is set amongst vineyards and banana plantations, at the foot of the La Orotava valley, and the people there are very friendly and welcoming. It is set amongst the backdrop of Mount Tiede, Tenerife's extinct volcano, which is almost always snow-capped, despite the year round temperature of 22-30 degrees.

Gill Yardley

BANDBOX

Faded memories of gob stop kissing and sucked in cigarettes,
Peeling paint and harshly turned wood,
Splinters lodged in the palm of your hand.
Palm Sunday crosses and
Cenotaph wreaths.
The Bandstand.

Guzzled cider.
Foam frothing sweetness,
drip fattened chips,

Newspaper wrappings,
Swirling in a leaf breeze,

Heat baked mud ponds, crossed with ease.
Sun dried dog turds kicked with abandon
Rusted metal scraping on the child's swing
Discordant Symphony.

Morning Dew dried hay
And cast aside,
A groundsman's bucket,
Leaching chalk onto the bolted ground.

Petticoats lifting, with a glimpse of knicker.
Plump breasted and clutched in tightly..

Solemn oaths made with penknives
Scratched on bench
held for ever.

The warm embracing darkness descending on us,
like a slow fog,
in its slow wrapping,
warm wrapping
stealth wrapping Nightness.

Safe now,
From the Grown Ups.

Simon Grenville

THE BLACK-HEADED GULL

There is a tale about an old woman, a writer, who lived on the coast and wrote at night with a candle burning. On her desk she kept scrolls of thin paper and a small porcelain vase that she used for an inkpot. The shelves of her little house were stuffed with driftwood, pebbles, smooth bones and shells gathered from the beach. On the windowsill she kept a collection of gleaming bird skulls alongside her most prized possession, a small Aeolian harp that issued an ethereal hum as the wind passed through it. Because she lived alone, preferring the company of birds and animals to humans, some viewed the old woman with suspicion and there were rumours of witchcraft.

As she emptied sand from her shoe after her walk one morning, the old woman saw a basket on the doorstep with a note that read, "To the bird lady, please accept this small gift." How kind! She looked all around but saw no one. Once inside, she cleared away the paper, the candle and the porcelain vase, put the basket on the desk and pulled back the cloth to find some eggs — seven altogether. One much larger and bluer than the others. How curious! Certainly not a hen's egg. How did it get there? The old woman picked up the egg, weighing it in her palm. It was warm. She went to the kitchen window, gazed into the clear blue sky and back to the egg in her hand. After a moment's thought she took off her hat, gently placed the egg inside, and set it down on a chair near the fireplace.

Next day, just before dawn, the egg cracked and out came a ruffled grey seagull chick. Its hungry chirping woke the old woman, who had been dozing at her writing desk. Surprised, she looked for something to give the chick, and found bread and some ginger cake. She mothered the gull until some days later when it vanished through the window, returning most days to eat bread from the windowsill. Over the coming months the old woman noticed with delight that on breezy days the bird spent much longer on the sill, apparently bewitched by the humming of the harp.

They say that one morning, about a year after finding the basket, the old woman dozed off and never woke up again, and when the gull appeared there was nothing for it to eat. It hopped over to the old woman, who was slumped across the writing desk. It brushed its head against her cheek and pecked the back of her cold hand. Getting no response, it flew into the kitchen and began rummaging through bottles, packets, boxes and jars. Finding nothing, it flapped from shelf to shelf, picking and prodding between the bones and shells, before hopping back to the desk and dipping its head into the porcelain vase. When the head emerged from the vase it was covered in black ink, as if in mourning.

That night there was no wind and the sea was still. Returning late from shore leave, two sailors saw the kitchen window standing open. They peered into the silence. They called out, and, sensing easy pickings, they brushed aside the harp and the bird skulls and climbed into the dark house. Once inside they lit a match. The flame illuminated the dead eye of the old woman at the desk as a ghost-white bird emerged from the gloom. Blackness again filled the house as the spent match dropped to the floor and the men backed away, tiny bird skulls cracking beneath their feet. Although the head of the phantom bird was missing, it somehow issued a piercing screech that grated horribly with the frenzied cries of the sailors.

They say that at first light two corpses were discovered on the beach beneath a great flock of screaming gulls, their hair having turned completely white. The body of the old woman was never traced and, even to this day, some of the locals swear that if you stand for long enough on that spot you will hear the Aeolian harp humming around the cove.

Russ Berry

AS IF THEY KNOW

When I see my reflection
in the burnished copper of your eyes
I wonder is it me you see?
Or are the images in your head
of your kin,
falling
bones breaking
skin tearing
flesh burning.

You stand so still
as I caress the soft suede of your skin,
just an twitch of your ear as I whisper your name.
Did you hear them too?
The screams of men
of their bones breaking
skin tearing
flesh burning
how their flesh burned.
And now within this agony called war
it is as if you know,
you draw close,
nudge me softly,
warm, familiar, musky.
I see my reflection
as I touch the cold steel against your head.

Then I close our eyes.

Jo Roberts

MUSE

Recently I got to thinking about what inspires those who write? Where do their ideas come from? I suppose I should also ask, "how long is a piece of string?" — Everyone is different.

However, I am truly fascinated by the genesis of an idea, and can remember as a young child reading the *Garden Gang* books, written by 7 year-old Jayne Fisher, about Percival Pea and Polly Pomegranate or Penelope Strawberry and Roger Radish. I remember reading an article about her and where she got her ideas from that fascinated me. I was astounded that a girl near my age was writing and was published; that was amazing to me, it is something that has stayed with me ever since. Where do ideas come from?...

In the years since, I have often thought of and been fascinated by that compulsion to go and create, make something from thoughts and imagination – how does it happen? — to me it's magical. I have even read an article or two about a published author's own reasons for writing – Murakami, James Herbert etc.

Music is often a source of inspiration and there are many who have written as a result of being inspired to some degree by music. Or there are those who, having been inspired, write music or songs.

Chris Martin (from the band Coldplay) wrote the song *Fix You* for his then-wife Gwyneth Paltrow, however their marriage was not meant to be and they are now in the process of 'conscious uncoupling'. Perhaps she was his muse for a while, and they say often heartbreak leads to great art.

Taylor Swift is well known for writing about the break-ups with her ex-boyfriends in songs also. In some instances her muse (in the sense of a source of an inspiration) has been a boy / man – how refreshing.

There is, in the public domain and the common psyche, the stereotype of the artist with his muse (often a woman) and, historically, it is common knowledge in arts and mythology that a muse — that which gives an artist inspiration — is often depicted as a woman.

The dictionary definition of muse is as follows:

In Classical Mythology
a. Any of a number of sister goddesses, originally given as Aoede (song), Melete (meditation), and Mneme (memory), but latterly and more commonly as the nine daughters of Zeus and Mnemosyne who presided over various arts: Calliope (epic poetry), Clio (history), Erato (lyric poetry), Euterpe (music), Melpomene (tragedy), Polyhymnia (religious music), Terpsichore (dance), Thalia (comedy), and Urania (astronomy); identified by the Romans with the Camenae.
b. any goddess presiding over a particular art

For me, muse means that which causes inspiration and that can be anything. Anything can trigger that spark of inspiration, that magic which leads one to writing. I know they are not writers but often I think of the wonderful women I have heard of, some in my own family and some who are not, who were denied the opportunity to follow their heart's desire, as society and convention had set them on another path.

My maternal grandmother was married at 14 years of age; she had no other choice, it was an arranged marriage in India. I have often wondered what she would have chosen to do if was given the right to choose. What I do know is that all her daughters went to university and became doctors.

The grandmother of a friend of mine was smart and able enough to get the grades to go to Cambridge to study medicine. However her family would not allow it, as it would be easier for her to marry if she became a nurse and so a nurse she became. This was back in the 1940's when she was a young woman and had her life ahead of her.

However her daughter was a scientist and her granddaughter did go to Cambridge and became a PhD, doctor and a scientist also.

This inspires me to write, it stirs something in me. There are many tales of missed opportunities out there and what could have been. Yet, equally, there are many stories of success, fulfilment and a life well lived

So many stories yet to be written, interesting and inspiring yarns, stories of every type and hue, being formed and on the verge of coming to life, breathed into being first by becoming thoughts and coming to life by being written down.

So what's your current muse? What inspires you? Are you doing anything about the muse that is whispering in your ear or pulling you in a certain direction to get something done?

I hope that you get to create that which is calling to you. As Lao Tzu (Chinese Philosopher) says, "A journey of a thousand miles begins with a single step".

As those far wiser than I have said, if you have any thought / desire to do anything go – "Explore, Dream, Discover" (Hemingway) and, for those of you who like words, "Keep writing!" (Jo Roberts).

Sukhmani Bawa

MADRIGAL

The chilling echoes of an era's end;
The life force of a new reformation,
An enlightened epoch,
with no end to claim.

An ode to unity,
With the human instrument
And no other.

Separated only by segments,
Which either individual or group
Rhythmically resonate.

David Hurt

MONOLOGUE: A WISH

The lyrics from the song by Great Big World and Christina Aguilera, Say Something (I'm Giving Up on You), *can be heard softly playing in the background.*

In my head, by the time I was 36 years old I had always pictured that I would have my beautiful wife and children with ruddy, chubby cheeks and soft hair ideal for ruffling, a dog and a cat and a house by the sea. Yes, that was supposed to be the life for me.

But for some reason I don't understand, try as I might, I am out there meeting women, but at the moment, all they all seem to want to be is my friend.

I hate those words, "let's be friends" and being relegated to the 'friend zone'; no guy wants a women he's attracted to say, "Let's be friends only". Those words make me want to bash my head against a terracotta flowerpot in despair.

I have no idea how my parents have managed to be happily married for over 27 years and still enjoy talking to each other, being in the same room as each other — astonishing. I usually am not that interested in what women have to say, to be honest. If it wasn't for my spreadsheet to keep track of who told me what, when, I would have no way of keeping track, as I don't remember such things.

I have so much love to give, in every sense, not just the obvious trite and physical way, and am so ready to be a father. I'd like to have a daughter and I'd call her May.

Sita, a good friend and old flatmate, said she was unsure whether the world was ready for me to have children. I told her, "Well, everyone had better buckle up and enjoy the ride." Sita laughed out loud when she heard that, I'm still not quite sure why.

All those thirty-something women – they should know by now that sex in your thirties is great, they just don't know what they are missing by not going out with me. I even told them that on the WhatsApp group

I'm a part of. I was a little upset at the time, but I am always true to myself and say what I feel. I just can't pretend for the sake of it.

I know what I'm missing and I'm desperate to have that back in my life — as the song goes, a true companion in every sense of the word. And, more than that, I like having someone to bother first thing in the morning.

I get terribly lonely being by myself. I only need four to five hours sleep — just think, I could be spending the other 20 hours a day with a very lucky lady. I do fill my time: I'm addicted to online gaming, it really occupies my time, and when I'm playing on my computer, I don't have to think about anything else. I like to shut the world out on a regular basis. Would be nice to have other options for doing this also; to be in love and have someone to have midnight sushi picnics with.

Why don't more women like online gaming? The perfect partner for me would be a woman who liked to play online games. That would mean she would understand if I wanted to go play *Elder Scrolls* or *Eve* on my computer for four hours straight and she wouldn't expect me to entertain her constantly.

Paula, she was beautiful (azure blue eyes, slender, five foot nine inches tall, a brunette with almost natural-looking dyed-blond hair). She heard me speaking in French in Canary Wharf. She was impressed that I did not swear continually in my conversation on the phone, as most men do when speaking in a foreign language.

I honestly thought that my luck was about to change, as Paula was the one who suggested to me that we should exchange phone numbers and that we should meet up again.

I thought she was amazing and true to her word. It was great to be in constant communication with her on Facebook and by text. Talking to women on the phone is way over-rated. On Facebook and text you can at least respond when you feel like it; at your convenience, not under the gun so-to-speak. To respond in real time you are on the spot a bit, when you speak on the telephone, I think. That way you also don't have to pretend to be interested in whatever they are saying. I barely pay attention to what they are saying, I much prefer when I'm doing the talking and they are listening to me.

I even changed from the Hammersmith office to the Canary Wharf office so that I could meet Paula for lunch in Covent Garden. I got round to asking her out on a date, but have had my share of excuses — especially recently — as to why a woman won't give me a chance or they go for the expensive meal and the opera but not want to see me again after that, or they say those magic words, "Let's be friends"

I didn't know whether to believe her, as I've heard the same excuse from another woman also (Alexa, the girl I liked before Paula was on the scene). 'The brush off.' When I asked her out, she was just so full of shit, I mean excuses, as to why she couldn't go out with me.

I much prefer Russian or Eastern European women; at least they are honest with you. I realise that Katerina, my last serious girlfriend when I was living in Berlin, only went out with me because I was a foreigner and was earning good money at the time. At least I had the opportunity to improve my German also, as she didn't speak good English. Paula said that she had broken up recently from a serious relationship and was not ready to date again at the moment. That's the same thing Alexa said, but I knew better than to believe Paula. I know now that in fact translates to mean they will sleep with the first fucking bastard Italian who happens to appears in their orbit. I don't understand; what does an Italian man have that I don't? They are not that special. The women I know seem to find Italian men irresistible.

That's what Alex and Paula did. I'll have to ask if he was Italian, her new 'friend'. I kind of have a feeling he was — I know my luck.

I was besotted with Alex, and treated her with respect and dignity and was willing to wait for her until she felt ready to date again. I spent over £760 on meals out, having to sit though the painful story of her marriage breakup and how her husband had cheated on her. But where did that get me? Within four days of meeting Fabio she was sleeping with the fucking bastard. I hate fucking bastard Italians.

Eric, an old friend from university, says why bother to go to all that trouble. That for £760 I could get all the sex I want in Thailand and a fully luxurious holiday. That is so not my style. Just the thought of paying for sex makes my skin crawl. I do have some standards, not many — but some.

It's good having Eric around with me in London. He was in Australia for the last five years and I was unable to see him as he didn't travel during that time. We both failed two years of our uni exams as we used to skip classes to play computer games. Sita thinks that Eric is creepy and that he needs many years of counselling.

We've both got a new interest: assembling, painting and playing battles with little miniature soldiers. It's great fun.

Sita, said it sounded well dodgy when I told her that two grown men were going to spend an afternoon playing with two 12 year-old boys. She said make sure that their mothers know where they are going and who they are with, just in case. All we were going to do is play with the miniature army battles in the toy shop. Sita couldn't stop laughing when I told her about it.

Eric likes Chinese, South-East Asian beauties mostly because they will listen to what he says. His ex-girlfriend got up at 3am after he got in from his bar shift, just so she could massage his feet for him and get him something to eat. That's the kind of woman he likes: someone who is compliant and easy to mould and will do what he says and who is not as intelligent as he is.

I would like my partner to work. I think women look great in office wear — well, if they are in shape, of course, to look good in and out of their clothes — and the ones who know how to dress. I like women who take care of themselves. I like women who wear makeup on their faces to make their skin look homogenous, and with strong, sexy Eastern European or Russian accents.

At Christmas and in the summertime I feel it very much, the absence of something that I lack. My family, my cousin and their happy children are a constant reminder of what they have and I lack. At times, I hate going home to see my happily close-knit family. I feel I have achieved some things in my life, but in other ways — relationship-wise — not much at all really. That really bothers me: it makes me feel inadequate and like there's something wrong with me. I don't think there is, but that's how I feel.

Time is seeping away. My mother has been ill: I do my best to go home when I can; not had a proper holiday in three years as am constantly going home to check on my mum and dad every month, and that is burning up all my holiday leave.

I feel like have achieved some things in my professional life, but I know that I'd like to have a partner and family. People say that I am stubborn and that I have to have things just as I want them when I want them. What I do know is I will have a family and children. It's not happened yet and I am in no rush, as I don't want to make the wrong decision. There are some women around but no-one who suits me in the way that I would like her to. I'd like her to play a musical instrument if possible and have a job which means she can follow me wherever or to whatever country I choose to live in, if I so choose.

Sometimes, since I came to England, I wish that it was somehow easier to meet women. Well, I have no problem meeting women, it's the question of getting them to go out with me. One's enough — and one just in case the first doesn't work out until we are a couple. That's not including the ones you only sleep with — friends with benefits or, as I like to call them as I'm open and honest, fuck buddies. Sita says try saying that to them and see whether they will let you sleep with them after that. She said most women like a little sophistication about a situation, irrespective of what it is. What does she know anyway about such things? She claims never to have had a one night stand anyway.

I'm a good catch: I have a car, and a holiday home in France and will have another house just as soon as I can afford it, even if it's not in London. I heard that recently the average price of a place in London is £409,000. How is that affordable on one person's salary? I do have another house in the south of France also, but that's an investment. There's no point in having a good job if there is no one to spend time with. I had a great job, but it ended, there was nothing for me in Derby. Life is amazing in London, and during the day I am occupied at work. But when you are with someone it makes everything better, it really does. London appears to be a good way to spend money.

So, what is it about England that is preventing me having a woman in my life? I am so ready to settle down. I'm as ready as it's possible to be. I've tried online dating, no words speed-dating and a range of meet-up groups and still they — every woman I meet — they all want to be friends. I am about ready to give up. Two beautiful women even looked me up on Facebook and wanted to stay with me, but they both slept on the couch, neither of the pretty blonde-haired and blue-eyed Russians wanted to share my bed with me. I don't understand: I am always there for people and am the go-to man for people when they are in trouble or want a favour, but to date no real sugar and nothing has matured into a relationship.

Sita says, her Australian mate, Aiden, whenever she stays over at his place, gives up his bed for her and he sleeps on the couch. I don't believe that men like that exist or they actually do that. Sita's known him for over 16 years and he always gives up his bed for her, so that show's he's a good guy apparently. I bet she's just saying that.

Eric, is not having any luck meeting a woman in London. What's going on? His pretty Chinese MBA study buddy came over to stay and he says even she slept on the couch and wanted to be "friends". Would be a completely different story if we were Italians!!

Sita says that I come across as desperate and that I should flow with things and let things happen naturally. If I followed her advice, I'd be unattached as she is. I don't understand what she means anyway. I have to be able to influence the situation or the circumstances somehow. She said something about listening to women when they speak and taking an interest in what they do and how they spend their time, what makes them tick, instead of talking about myself all the time. I'm not interested in what job they have, but what they do in their spare time. Sita said that may be so but if you remember what job she does, that indicates to her that that you are taking an interest in her and her life. That it's simple: just take an interest in her and her life.

Women like that apparently. Wonderful and unexpected dividends can result from taking a genuine and sincere interest in what a woman has to say, they are not a means to an end or baby factories / incubation units only.

My mother's getting old and I see her aging before my eyes. She's not as strong as she used to be, and her heart problems are leaching the life out of her body. Her eyes are still full of love and wonder when she sees me, but I know it's only a matter of time and she will no longer be around. Wouldn't it be something to be able to show her my child, I mean mine and my wife / partner's child? I know that would mean a lot to my parents. But it's more than that. Being with someone makes everything better. I told Sita that so many times but she doesn't seem to understand at all.

Sighing deeply as looks at the window (leaning against it, forehead on his forearm) as the song Say Something (I'm Giving Up on You) *continues to play in the background and can be heard more clearly now.*

Sukhmani Bawa

THE FUTURE OF AIR TRAVEL

Taking shape, unfolding on a powder blue counterpane,
Nimbus clouds; their saintly forms drifting into angel wings.

Gazing from their summer lawns, children mourn
The passing of the holidays,
They wonder at the skywriting:

We are burning the planet

Soon enough the contrails will be stripped of all their idylls,
Eternal rain will fall and fill the lawns with soft white feathers.

We will scrub away the layers of blue,
Scatter angel wing bones,
Cross out the sky.

Russ Berry

EPITAPH

In the town where I was born, it was expected that if you were male and of a certain age you would join the Royal Navy and serve your country. As children, all the games we played in the backstreets that weren't football were something to do with the sea. Pirates, or warships, or fighting sea monsters. At least that's how I remember my childhood. I enjoyed the games almost as much as everyone else, but 'almost' means it wasn't quite the same for me. That it was different, that I was different. Kids know when you don't quite fit in, when there's a little bit of a difference. They might not know how they know, or what the difference is, but they do know. That's when you get treated differently. I was always the prisoner captured by the pirates, or the giant squid to be chased and harpooned by the brave sailors. Very occasionally, if I was lucky, I would get to be a pirate for a while, or one of the sailors rowing the skiff carrying the harpoon. But they knew. They knew I didn't want to go to sea. They knew before I had even admitted it to myself, before the thought of doing anything else had occurred to me. My dad was an able seaman in the navy, my two elder brothers were sea cadets; how was it possible I could do anything else?

When I was in my last year at junior school I was chosen to sit the entrance exam for the local grammar school. My mum was enthusiastic and wrote a letter to my dad who had just left with his ship for an extended tour of duty to the Pacific. By the time his reply came back I had already taken the exam and been accepted for the school. Mum was quiet after she had read his letter, and said only that he was pleased I had been "given a chance". It was only much later, when I was leaving for university on a scholarship, that I found out the truth.

It first dawned on me at the start of my third year at the grammar school that I didn't want to be a sailor. I had joined the sea cadets when I started at my new school, and had been on several short boat trips. I found them exciting right up to the point where I couldn't see land. That's when I got violently seasick, and spent the rest of those trips with my head either over the side of the boat, or over a bucket. The sickness lasted until I set foot back on land. It got to the point where even the commanding officer started to recommend I didn't go on the longer trips. Before long I had left the sea cadets, and given up on a career in the Royal Navy. When my dad came home on leave he couldn't hide his disappointment about my decision, and I remember awkward silences and questions.

My happiest hours were when I was at the desk in the corner of the bedroom I shared with my two elder brothers. Here, I could escape into the books I had brought home from school and the local library. Here, I was the captain of the pirates not the prisoner, I was the one who fired the harpoon, I was completely in control of my imaginary life. The evenings passed quickly when I was in my room. When I received the scholarship to go to university it was as if a new door onto the world had been opened for me. The school had persuaded mum to apply and helped her to complete the apparently endless paperwork. She was, if anything, happier for me than I was for myself! Dad's view was much more downbeat, and on his next leave, I overheard them arguing more than once about what a sailor's son was doing going to university, with the toffs and nobs. I think that was when he gave up on me ever going to sea. I saw it in his eyes the day he went to rejoin his ship: the sense of loss, of confusion about my making choices he didn't like, and couldn't understand. I felt it in the cursory handshake and hug as he went out of the door. That was the last time I saw my dad, my last physical contact with him, the last touch.

We had no telephone then, and home was many miles away, so my only contact with mum was by letter. My parents wrote to each other every week while dad was at sea. Not long letters, but short letters telling each other of life's minutiae, keeping in touch. They would often arrive in small bundles with an elastic band around them. Mum and Dad had got into the habit of putting the date on the envelope so that they could be read in the correct order. None of his letters ever asked about university, they just included a hope I was happy. When I went away to university, Mum began writing to me every week with her news and snippets from my dad's letters she thought would interest me. My replies were less frequent, but as I recall it, I managed to reply at least once a fortnight.

War arrived in my second semester. There was no immediate call-up for us. We were told that as students of engineering, and especially as scholarship students, we would be exempted anyway. My dad had written a longer letter home. This time it had some lines blacked out. Everything hinting at his whereabouts had been censored. The letter was only allowed to say that he didn't know when he would be returning, he was safe, he missed us, and not to worry if we didn't hear for a while.

We hadn't heard from him for 10 weeks, and he had been away at war for 18 months when we got the official letter. I was home for the Christmas break when it arrived. It was a short letter. He was missing in action, presumed dead. His ship had been sunk whilst escorting a convoy. Doing his duty. These words speared me like the harpoons from my childhood, only this was no game, nor was it something I would or could ever forget. He had died doing his duty, while I was off with the toffs at university.

My mum begged me not to join up. My two elder brothers were already in the navy. I was her hope she said. But, as I left to return to university, my mind was made up. I think she knew, although she never said anything. After visiting my tutor to explain my reasons, I went to the recruitment office on the campus. I explained my problem. The officer wasn't fazed, he said many sailors were seasick at first, but there were jobs where it might not be a problem.

After twelve weeks of basic officer training, and numerous opportunities to demonstrate exactly how seasick I could be, I received my first posting as a second lieutenant. It was at sea, but not on the sea. I was to be a submariner, living and working under the sea. As it turned out we did spend long periods on the surface, charging batteries and changing the air, but these were most often at night, when we were less likely to be seen, and I found knowing I had a refuge where I couldn't see the horizon made all the difference. With time, my seasickness faded. My new responsibilities on the boat helped to push it down to insignificance. At long last, the war ended, and by some great stroke of fortune, both of my brothers and I survived, albeit with the scars that came from years at war. I resigned my commission as soon as it was allowed, and after a few months back at home, returned to university at the start of the next academic year to complete my degree.

This was all many years ago — a different life, a different world — but those few years as a submariner were the most formative of my life. They made me who I am, defined me, and, I felt, redeemed me in the eyes of my father, although he would never know it.

One of the few chances we have to choose how we are remembered by the future is our epitaph, chiselled deep into our headstone. I want mine to include the words, “Here lies a man who went to sea.”

Keith Hands

THE PLAYERS

I know so much about the foolish players,
that play in love's wise playing fields.

That's why my eyes stay foolishly open,
while my lips are wisely sealed.

David Louis

INSPIRATIONS

The Dark Side of Blackie *by David Louis* — inspired by music.

The Carnival *by Keith Hands* — inspired by the song *The Carnival is Over.*

Bedevilled by Buttons *by Gill Yardley* — inspired by the song *Frosty the Snowman.*

Loaded *by Russ Berry* — inspired by the music of Primal Scream.

Sweet Memories *by Elizabeth Draper* — inspired by the song *Memories are Made of This.*

The Day the Wall Came Down *by Simon Grenville* — inspired by the music of the theatre.

Entrance to a Wood *by Russ Berry* — inspired by the music of nature.

It's Beginning to Look a Lot Like Christmas *by Christine Marsh* - Inspired by the song *It's beginning to look a lot like Christmas*.

Born Without a Twin *by Sarah Menary* — inspired by the song *The Heart is Hard to Find.*

Master of the Metal String *by Anna Bradley* — inspired by the music of family.

Poetry in Motion by *Harminder Sihota* — inspired by Elvis.

A Grace Note *by David Louis* — inspired by the music of the festive season.

Writer's Block *by Sarah Meany* — inspired by the song *Writer's Block.*

The Audition *by Caroline Duffy* — inspired by the beauty of the voice.

The Tapestry Child *by Elizabeth Draper* — inspired by the song *Tapestry.*

A Small White Envelope *by David Deanshaw* — inspired by the song *Love Letters.*

Moon *by Jo Roberts* — inspired by the song *Blue Moon.*

Musical Taste *by Jo Roberts* — inspired by the classics.

The Hills were Alive *by Elizabeth Draper* — inspired by the musical *The Sound of Music.*

Beethoven Symphony Within *by David Hurt* — inspired by Beethoven's 9th Symphony, and his *Eroica.*

Sax *by David Hurt* — inspired by the iconic sound of Jazz, and the saxophone's influence on it.

Burn Baby Burn *by Gill Yardley* — inspired by the song *Burn Baby Burn.*

Bandbox by Simon Grenville — inspired by a bandstand.

Black-headed Gull *by Russ Berry* — inspired by music of the sea.

As if they Know *by Jo Roberts* — inspired by song of *As if They Know*

Muse *by Sukhmani Bawa* — inspired by The Band Muse.

Madrigal *by David Hurt* - inspired by the end of the Renaissance and the start of Modernity, and by the sounds of the voices of a madrigal.

Monologue: A Wish *by Sukhmani Bawa?* — inspired by the song *Say Something*.

The Future of Air Travel *by Russ Berry* — inspired by imagining the complete silence of a post-apocalyptic world.

Epitaph by Keith Hands— inspired by The Beatles song *Yellow Submarine*.

The Players *by David Louis* — just inspired.

32758075R00042

Made in the USA
Charleston, SC
25 August 2014